The Perfect Place to Pray

Daughter of Zion

Angel Clove

The Perfect Place to Pray

ISBN: 978-1-945976-56-8

Library of Congress Control Number: 2019916128

Published by EA Books Publishing a division of Living Parables of Central Florida, Inc. a 501c3

EABooksPublishing.com

Acknowledgments

I would first and foremost like to thank my Lord and hero Jesus Christ; my all in all! I thank you Jesus for your gifts, and for not forsaking me. I thank you Jesus for a second chance at life, and for always being there for me, even when I was filthy and in the grave. Thank you, Jesus for using me. Thank you for even looking at me and determining that I could bare the privilege of being called your child. I thank you Jesus for cleaning me and making me new again. I know that this is only the beginning, but I am riding until the wheels fall off. I will enjoy this journey all the way until we meet again.

I am so grateful for my family; my all, my sunshine, my sunset, my sunrise, and my sunny days. My husband Algernon, Nivea, Aniyah, Noah, and Nia. They are the best things that have ever happened to me. They are hilariously full of life, and character that keeps me going. They make me so proud each day.

Also, I would like to acknowledge Hattie Glee, she has made such an impact in my life. She has been used greatly by the Lord to help mold me in a very pivotal point in my life. She also has been very helpful in my children, and husband's life. I would like to acknowledge my mother in law for her helpful hands, and for her fervent prayers. Also, all of my family in St. Louis, I love you all. Thank you also to all of my brothers and sisters in the Body of Christ.

Throughout these pages are some quotes, emotions, thoughts and feelings. All are what I either believed, thought, or hoped for in my life. Some things that I believed the Lord to have spoken to me at one time are what I believe, or believed during that time in my life. Some things could have been felt by emotions, some things may not have been Jesus; just solely what I felt or what I believed. Anything that is not for you, or not so in your life do not receive. Read with an open heart, and with understanding. Let the Lord minister to you with what he says is so.

Enjoy

Table of Contents

Introduction

I sometimes find myself staring off lost in thought remembering the times when I used to dream. Even my dreams weren't really dreams, just pieced together portraits of what I had seen. I was a child with no hope; seemingly a lost cause always looking for a step that would lead me to a place of happiness. I realized at a young age that the road to happiness was strenuous, detrimental, and fatal. I had to die to live again, be born again to be invited on a journey with the Lord. This journey would take me too many different unforeseen trials, and test. Still I only had a minimal understanding of who Jesus was in me. I was no longer seeking my own qualities, but I was coming to the divine realization of the true essence that lies within.

The Holy Ghost has broken the barriers of thoughts I used to have, and has opened me to the contemplation points of the Lord. I have understanding now that I am not seeking a peace from within, I am solely seeking a piece of him.

When God quenches the urge with his presence; I come back humbly pleading for the revelation of who he has created me to be for him. My cries go up yearning for the Lord to be pleased. Life quickly tries to alter the perception of my circumstances in the life that I was dealt. I am left with no other alternative but to trust, and to plead for the Lord to forever be present. Everyone else has left, taken the easy way out, abandoned and misused all that the Lord has placed within his daughter. What the others have misused God has used. So, I invite you to come and enter into this sacred place of understanding the perfected outcome of great suffering.

Chapter 1

Trials

Trials - Purposeful test of mighty acts that draw you nearer to God.

Time after time thoughts have tried to become my outcome becoming heavy weights tugging away at my mind; trying the presence of God in me. Who am I? Am I good enough? Who will I be when I grow up? In this place, none of those things even matter. Who am I becoming he is, am I good enough becomes perfected peace. Who will I be when I grow up becomes everlasting eternity that doesn't counts the days of your youth. Eternity holds fast the continuation of what can be in the hope of his revealing. Quickly the peace comes, but I have learned to yield because as it comes it is sealed. It is sealed in the depths of the Lords womb only used for a time such as this. Once it has been given by the Lord it is placed in the area of need so the needs are no more. Everything is fulfilled, nothing is broken all is recovered and victory shows up as is. Strife comes seeking the piece that has been given, that you may not even know you had. Now you are not even desiring anything of God. Even your desires are made manifest by it coming up before your heart.

I have faced many trials never realizing that the Lord Almighty's footsteps were very much present with me. Jesus walked beside me only to one day walk in me. His hopes may have been that I would receive his hope. One day becoming destitute to all the things that I once knew before him. Yielding to his everlasting life.

I remember a time when I went to Nashville Tennessee for New Years, back then I didn't have the Holy Ghost. I believe that during this time the presence of the Living God was preparing me. Preparing me for the weaning off of this realm into the entry ways of his eternal salvation.

I remember being in a hotel with my now husband. I didn't drink much as I watched him consume more and more liquor. As we exited the hotel room we gathered into a huge crowd of people headed to see the Nashville ball drop. I remember my fiancé's mood shift, and I felt in my spirit to turn and go back. I turned and we let go of one another. When I looked back the crowed had consumed the space between him and I, and immediately he was gone. My chest began to pound with fear not realizing what had just happened. Naturally I didn't know why it had happened, or how to find my way back to him. It was divine purpose, all a part of Gods perfect will over my life.

As I stood separating myself from the crowd looking for him, the very him I was really looking for found me. At that very moment, I had chosen to walk with God. I fearfully walked as his Angels guided me leading me to safety. Jesus maneuvered me to a designed destination, and I had no idea I had even arrived. I frantically asked for help trying to call for who could hear, using the cell phone of a stranger, and flagging down police. No one seemed to notice my plea. An officer told me to catch a bus that would be taking off for people who had been drinking that didn't want to drive. I found the bus and hesitantly got on. I sat with strangers watching the infamous ball being dropped and hearing the time shouted. I didn't realize that the time was quickening my soul to know that time would soon be no more. The time had come for me to come closer to the Kingdom of God. As the bus drove off, my location was never announced. I had no set place, and I didn't even ask. I just rode, being led all along by the spirit of the Living God. The bus stopped and everyone was escorted off. We all stood in a line, and I grew fearful as onlookers watched me seek my fiancé and ask for help. Strangers came peeking and sizing up my physical attire, but all along it was the devil watching the anointing being sifted. I may have seemed misplaced then, but I was being found by God in that very moment. A petite lady noticed me and offered me a ride with a selected few. I had no phone, no money, and no recollection of where my hotel was. I was terrible with directions, and couldn't help but realize how clueless I was. Nevertheless, the Alpha and Omega had my steps directed and paved right before him.

As I sat in the back of a small van, I looked over as we ventured onto the highway. I looked out of the window shocked, suddenly spotting my fiancés jacket. I realized it was him the one I had lost. Only by the hand of God was I led to look and see my fiancé standing at a gas station. I quickly caught the driver's attention and I told her, "It's him!" The driver pulled off the road and offered my fiancé a ride as well. We made it back to the hotel, saddened and afraid I cried out to the Lord like never before. I screamed for God to protect us, and to not let anything happen to us. I was very overwhelmed by this experience, only to realize that this wasn't an experience but a divine interaction with God. This was the building of a new relationship, one that God himself desired to continue for all my days.

Trials come to test, demanding by God to enter into the place of comfort to stir you to a place of divine reckoning. Trials desire the will of God to come forth, even though we resist. That was one experience, but there were more calling out for me after that.

I look back at a time when I was in college, no goals just knowing that I had to finish so I could accomplish something. The road to accomplishment in that place was such a challenge. Even though I was there, I was still grieving my new place and suffering in the old place. I finished college with my associate's degree only to face many challenges, and roadblocks. While extending my courage to receive a bachelor's degree, I got close to the dream of actually making it. Unfortunately, trials called me by name once more, being divinely sent by God to draw me.

All of the doors that were once opened seemed to close at once. I thought my diligence to fight for what I desired came from God but it was really opposition. It was really not knowing the ways of God. How can I plan a life that is not my own? How can I serve a purpose of what I desire when God created me to fulfil the desire of his heart?

How can I come to his purpose when I had not even known that it was him drawing me all along? God knew and it was perfect to him. God was never moved by the opposition that rested on me. God knew that at a divine time the plans of heaven would be done in earth. God knew that I would be sitting here in this very moment being used to do this very thing; fulfilling the righteousness of God for all that he created me for.

The doors had been closed there. I tried my best to finish school only having obtained an associate degree, with intentions of obtaining my bachelor's. The course curriculum had changed and other things stood in the way making the situation seem option less. Ultimately, I ended up moving to a whole other state. I yielded to the fact that there was no more in the place that I was in. It had become a dry place, a place that would no longer provide nourishment for what God had intended. Most importantly it seemed to have been the Lord who dried it up. When I moved I had no plan, no understanding of what all would unfold in this place; but surely Jesus did. The Lords grip was so heavily upon me there was no need to pray for the yoke to be broke he was my yoke, my band, my all. I still did not attend school I just became a stay at home mother, and a wife. All while I sat, my spirit man pleaded for me to come closer. I didn't know what the Lord was seeing in me and I never thought to ask. I just walked blindly, knowing that if the Lord is with me nothing else stood a chance.

Chapter 2

Pressures of Life

Pressure - Withstanding of righteousness only to come to the yielding of what can be by the letting go of what was!

Where do I begin? Pressure has made me face many things such as; vengeance, hate, lust, hurt, and even sadness. Pressure is when things are going smoothly but then out of nowhere a family member dies, or your husband is caught cheating. Now you seemingly heal and go on with life, but if you don't face what these events in your life caused it creates hidden hurts. Hidden angers, and insecurities hid deep inside of you. In my case I had a breakup and then quickly I met someone new. All of those hidden things came out on him and I had to be healed. All of these pressures could be sent by God only for the uprooting of the hidden things. The hidden things cling to the realm of the inner belly. These things seek the manifestation of God -like things so it can mimic and imitate Jesus in our lives. They pretend to manifest themselves as the real us but they don't belong to us, they are just experiences we have faced. These things never come to the pureness of the will of God, but their efforts are to taint the things that are. So, for example; a spouse is caught being unfaithful it hurts you, you leave him, and move on with your life. Even though you have moved on this interaction has planted a seed of hurt in you. The enemy plays on that seed, sometimes without you noticing it. Sometimes a person will say I don't date those types of men their cheaters. Really what has happened? That type of man may be your husband, but fear makes you afraid of being hurt again. The Lord uses these types of life experiences to let you know that he is God. Also, God uses the situation to heal you from hurt, and distrust by you having to face the truth. Once you face what is God can open the wound and place healing ointment in it. The ointment can be through prayer, or even worship. Nobody said that life is easy and that it doesn't occur, because we were created to have choice. God is there to free you from everything life's brought to you, and to keep you whole. All the while knowing that he is yours and you are his, he is God alone. All of this so you can have a real relationship with Jesus Christ, and know that he cares. Pressures of life wean us and stretch us to a point of no return. The stretching is simply for us come into the understanding that we must let the hidden things go. God will expect us to bring up a pure offering to him which is the pureness of our whole man (Mind, body, and soul). Being set free of the old man which is the thing that the kingdom of God will sanctify and seal. The new man then comes and alleviates the pain, even from the pressures that God sent to be the healing of old wounds. Also for the purifying of the things that abided in you!

Life's pressures are only for a time, they were never intended to hold us. They are solely for us to hold it, so we can give it back to who sent it. We a lot of times think, "Oh that's the enemy." What we should know is that the Lord made the enemy in hell and the ones portrayed in our everyday lives. He or they are not to harm one hair on our head. Everything God sends the enemy to do works only for our good; if we are children of the Most High God. We are his children so things that trouble us such as pressures he willingly takes them from us in due season. We have to know it was only for a season. Pressures bring us to the callings that God has placed upon us. The call is for all, the chosen are predestined as Gods elect. Who can lay a charge upon us, who but God? But with his charge comes greatness.

I had never seen myself as great and a lot of that was the problem. I sat holding onto pressures as if they were me, my very existence, but this was not so. I couldn't let them go because it had become all I had known. Being misused and being broken became a system for me. It became a way of living that was unhealthy for me, and all those that entered into the space that I was in. I knew nothing healthy or right I just knew how to hold on. I've learned that holding on was of God, but what I learned to hold onto through life was not. It was the trick of many things that would seek after Gods daughter. The pressures of life tried try to destroy the birthing that is taking place right now. As I type this very sentence, in this moment be encouraged because something is being birthed even in you... Right now!

Nothing could have hurt worse than knowing my full potential had been there at the feet of God all along, but I was not present along with the presenting of it all to him as one. Whoa that hurt! The purpose came to him, but I didn't come up to it. I stood in the shadows hiding in the fear of God exposing, and revealing the holding of my experiences. That alone is pressure in itself. God spoke one word and it was brought to its knees as the Holy Ghost in me was able to stand.

As the Holy Ghost came forth before God the Lord of Host ushered my soul into deliverance, brought my mind to the eternal, and called my spirit to acknowledge and receive all that God had planned for me. It wasn't too late, it wasn't out of reach, Michael (the arch angel) came and slayed the very essence of the hiding place. Grace spoke the True Essence of God over me for the protection of never going back!

I'm no longer afraid to reach, to lean on the understanding being brought up in me but not the ways of this natural realm. I had grown so used to it but no more! I have places to be and people to see, I have a destiny! Pressures tried to keep hold of me. Pressures tried blinding me in that I couldn't see what was, and by not seeing what was I couldn't see what could be. God said, "If only you will open your eyes and see all you mean to me. Empty yourself before me and yield to my call, yield to my ways, yield to the choice of my choosing to call you up by my name. YIELD!!!" I heard the declarations and my feet were quickened, I turned to run but I am more than a conqueror. I whispered boldly in my soul, "Jesus can you help me to be strong?" Instantly I felt strength come, muscle built and the heart beat was like the sound of drums. The sound of the drums was like a quickening, as their beaten urging the understanding to know that something Great has come! "New life! Give her new life, a fresh start in being all, extend time on her and let her be!"

I gasped as the Almighty decided right then and there to let loose on me all of what lied in his heart for me. In that moment, I had to become one with his vision. I was losing myself and coming to the overall understanding of what God intended. Not just what he intended for me, but what he intends to do through me for all that are assigned to me. It has nothing to do with me. The pressures were loosed and so was God, opening my eyes to see what I once couldn't.

As Dr. Martin Luther King said, "I have a dream," he may have once been in this place. Possibly he heard the same drums I heard knowing that whatever happens, "Greater is he that is in me than he who is in the world (1John 4:4 KJV)." No more fear, no more worry, the Lord inherited those who were suppressed by the vision, opening their eyes to something much greater. I could hear the Lord speaking in his might, "Come and see what it is, loose the pressures of vision and see what it is that I see!" No longer bound, no more chains on me, praise the Lord Hallelujah I see…

I was in a relationship so blind to my own worth, my value was dictated on the amount of what others saw, not of what I seen in myself. When confidence showed itself, it was a false façade of vanity and ego. I never knew the confidence of nothing else matters. I only knew the safety and comfort of my love ones which were few. The relationship that I was in was quickly stirred up with lust, dysfunction, and tender emotion. I had no idea of who I was or what God had called me to be. I was so in love with the man that I couldn't see the attacks were specifically designed for the destruction of the purpose that I have in the earth.

I was weak and fragile trying to be strong. I look back on times when I was cheated on and abused, but even in that place great affection remained in me. This time in my life was building me to a greater compassion, but not for the man. I was being tried to have a perfect heart before God.

I can recall being so insecure of other women and being so frail with worry of what will come of this? As time went on the spirit of the Lord brought me to my knees. I didn't know of him well back then, but because I'm his I knew enough to kneel and ask Jesus to help me. That simple prayer turned things around. This relationship had become a pressure too much for me to bear. I didn't know then but it was not meant for me to carry long term. Shortly after that prayer the Lord delivered me. A murder took place and the person that I was involved with in that relationship was arrested. In the wee hours of the night a knock on my door came. It was a friend of mine, frantically warning me to gather my belongings and my children. The man that I was involved with had killed someone and I was in great danger because of the status of who he had killed. It was a case of self-defense and the man that I was involved with was released from custody. I grabbed my children and stayed with that friend for the night. It was such a lifting from God, who would have known that God had that in mind?

The witnessing of a move of God; unfortunately, someone's child, brother, father, or son was taken. If you are in the will of God you understand that Lord heard the cry of his child in the earth in great distress, and troubled. I didn't have ears to hear then but I believe the Lord answered and said, "Suffer it to be so for now. For the righteousness of God must be fulfilled, but surely vengeance is mine saith the Lord!" Surely it was, that knock came not from a friend but it came from the one true King of Kings. The Glory of the Living God came and rescued me. That knock said to me, "The time is now that this pressure be lifted and be no more, let nothing stand in the way less it be cast down."

After that time, I went into transition… Most people are not aware that after deliverance the transition is revealed. The circumstances still may look familiar to you even though there has been a shift. The shift is the freeing of the pressures. In the transition you must be placed, healed and carried to the next place. You cannot just get there you have to endure the readiness of Gods plan. During this time frustration can come as the new pressure. Even though hurt and insecurity are no more, frustration and hate quickly can come in trying your faith towards God. The heavy weight of sadness and pain came to perfect your love. This comes to test your faith and bring forth a pure trust in God that if he did it already he will finish it!

Chapter 3

Transition

Transition - The heavy place.

The transition is the heavy place because this is what the spirit man feels while occupying this realm. It is so detrimental that you make it here. If you can see it's like you are on a journey in a desert. The circumstances are dry, and death seeking. You can't turn back because if you turn back it will be worst. The only thing that is worse than the transition is the remnant of the pressures you just escaped. So, you decide to look ahead, there is no other choice but to bear the conditions or die! There is no going back God speaks even in the deserted place saying, "My beloved in whom I am well pleased. Faithful in little so shall I be faithful in much; come sup with me (Luke 16:10 KJV)." In this place, your faith is stirred because your natural man only feels the circumstance not the voice, but if you hear and hearken you will see day. As you come to a place of fainting you stand saying, "I can make it!" No not so, in this place when you truly make it you fall. You fall so hard in that desert, lips destroyed from thirst, body completely deteriorated. If you are foolish enough to say I can do this you have not heard nor understood the will of God. "Not by might, nor by power, but by my spirit (Zechariah 4:6 KJV)." The length of time is then extended in this transitional place. If you fall giving way to the brittleness of the bones, and die utterly the Lord then breaths upon you. The Lord whispers in the declarations of his might, "You have made it." You stand by the lifting of the angels that were sent to bear with you all along so you never could have died even if you wanted to. The Lord of Host just wanted you to understand, not my will Lord but yours be done. The Lord desires you to depend solely on him. You look and see green pastures, the place that the Lord has named is the wilderness. Transition brings us to the desired place but you can't see what God desires unless you suffer for him to understand how to reign with him (2 Timothy 2:12 KJV).

In this time, I could not just say I'm free, see because of my foolishness a mess was made. A choice was made, that prayer changed it all for me. My ex and I were no longer in a relationship, but still very much connected. I was in a position to yield until the desired place was ready. I was so frustrated that I had these ties to this person that I didn't hate but was ready to be done with. A mess had been made that the Lord began to clean up. I had children, a home, and ties with this man in my life. My ex could have been called by God as well as us all, but for the chosen there can be no hindrance to what we were sent here to do. We are required to return home in the perfected state we were created in. God had to turn some things around. I began to be encouraged and strengthened. All of the sudden the desire for that man was taken from me and the interest and affections were no more. The ties had been cut. Bruises began to heal and the fear of what would come of this was no more.

There was a time I would jump at the sound of aggression but by the grace of God during this time I welcomed it! "Come on with it," was just what I felt, whatever will be will be I will not run! My ex's mood and demeanor was like a battered veteran shocked by what had occurred; being that close to death. My demeanor had changed too, shocked by being this close to life! All of the people that I hung out with were separated, it was a clique a big group and this event changed it all. One of my best friends would barely welcome me, the people that treated me with favor at one time turned their noses up in judgement. I decided to go shopping, I dressed myself, and I smiled still not realizing that God was at work. I had abandoned my home, and all of my belongings. I stayed with my ex's parents receiving their help with the children. I used to be afraid to drive only having a permit and nothing else; no one had ever taught me how to drive. Courage came to me though, I began paying attention to my directions, and I started to travel. I wasn't worried anymore of what could happen. I was happy yet frustration and anger were the hidden things, and ultimately this is what takes place. We think I'm happy, I'm okay, but really, we are in the pain of coming to these things. The bitterness that is lingering in the belly has no joy but we just go with what seems rather than yielding to the pain.

If I have been delivered I am free, but when you are delivered you are at peace to hear from God. Then you can let what is in the inward man that is not like him surface. When it comes up for the purging we swallow the vomit not wanting the unattractiveness of the filth that's in us to taint the cute exterior we have falsely established to come on us. "I'm not going back I'm happy now, I aint dealing with nothing else." Really at this point you are just beginning to heal. You have to understand that when God says heal there is something you have to be healed from. If you are delivered from hurt you don't begin to praise you come into to worship. It is there you find out what hurt you. Now you can be covered in safety to not receive that hurt again, and then you are healed. Nobody wants to face this, what really hurt you is you!

Blame is much easier, but it is you that resisted and denied Gods place in you. Even still you grow to the understanding of how it went wrong and where. Only now having to do what it is that you were made to do so that this will not be your rest.

That happiness I felt surely was vain it wasn't of God it was of the heathen. It was a false sense of I'm okay. Then came the clubs, tattoos, and the sobering after effect of what had been done. I began to grow weary of this time and decided to do right. I was so tired of not having what belonged to me, and being a house guest when I had already had my own. See what I had possessed materialistically wasn't built on a sturdy foundation and it was not established by the Most High. So, like the story of the Three Little Pigs (Galdone, P.G.J.C (2011). The Lord huffed and puffed and blew the house down.

I was resting on the couch having to share it with the one I had already been delivered from and I thought, "I am sick of this, this is so uncomfortable, why do I have to go through this?" "This is not my fault!" This was the yielding to the purging, if you can hear the mess begin to come up! I said to myself, "You know what I'm going to go get my stuff. I am going back to my house, and I am not going to be bothered with no gangbangers killing me. I'm about to get what's mine." I drove over to the house at night not realizing that there had been men watching the house, looking to catch a glimpse of us to redeem the loss of their love one. But what they didn't realize was that my redeemer was with me and Jesus died for me on the cross. I am in his flock and he would go to hell to keep from losing me or any others that belong to him!

I parked down the street and watched carefully as I stepped up to the house. I walked in the house and seen that the doors were all kicked in, the windows were all opened, papers were shuffled, and much was stolen. I looked in amazement at every door and window being pried; it had to have been many that entered in but by his grace. I went to go collect my clothes and seen that they were gone; almost everything was gone. I cried at the reality of how severe this act of God was. I couldn't do anything but turn around and leave. I started to come to the understanding that I have to come through this. After pressing on I eventually ended up finding an apartment, and for what I could afford.

My daughters were born prematurely, each one weighing at and under 1 pound, but completely healthy. The state awarded me with social security payments in my name. Because of this I was able to live on my own and start school. I had been restored, and I prepared for the move. Even though my ex's family had previously urged me to stay I politely said, "I have to go." The things were stolen but my soul was not, the Lord showed me that stuff was not his provision it was the reward of the wicked. The Lord said to me, "I will balance and keep you, let me provide for thee." I had one couch, and a bedroom set I was able to purchase for my children. My mistakes cost but see God did not suffer the little ones. They were in comfort while I rested in his safety. I didn't have much but I had more than enough. I looked around realizing, "Ahhh I had almost died in the struggle, but Jesus breathed upon me and I came into the desired place!!!" I had to go through the reality of what had been done so I could never go back. I was led to face what had been going on all along. I had to see what sought after his seeds. Everything was destroyed but nothing could be lost. God wanted me to be a witness to the testimony of what great measures he will go to to bring you out. Also, this revealed how close we all come to death in the spirit. Unfortunately, some are never able to be led by God. Being shown just how close you really came, and what it looks like in the natural. It's not the place it is the spirit of reality, the reality is that I was being destroyed to a point of death.

Nevertheless, God said, "You must live... LIVE>."

Chapter 4

The Destination

The Destination - This is not your rest.

Going through is only coming to, it doesn't mean that you have actually gone through. Even when you go through things you come to a place of feeling like you made it. Really God has only just begun. You have been saved by his might, but then his grace is sufficient enough to extend to the detrimental circumstances that you were in no matter how big.

The reality is now that you have been healed, now you have to be taught so you can grow. Being taught is the easy part it is easy to learn, being told every aspect of what to do. It is the growing to those things sought after by God that becomes the trial. Can I make it? This becomes the reality, because there is no going back, the past is erased all before this is irrelevant. It made you come here so you keep it, but it is kept in God not in you. Your sins are no more remembered but your suffering was recording never lost; you can actually give it to him. When you give up your experiences you actually give it all. You give the experience, and the suffering the experiences brought you to. The Lord separates the two, he cast down the remembrance of the hurt and sees it no more. Jesus cures the building up of the new, and releases the pressures all the while holding on to the testimony that it brought. So, at the right time God will call it up out of himself through you, only to declare for the removal of the pressures of your brethren. He is the deliverer but we belong to him so he brings us to a place of knowing that through him we can be delivered, but deliver as well.

There is no more attachment to the testimony, no tears that come with it unless it's tears of thanksgiving. No more tears of sorrow when you are really healed. You desire to bless others with what you came to not what you came through. This is why it is not your rest solely because you must go through the rest. That was only a percent of what God is able to do. That's not even accounting the percent of how much, but the accounting of how great and mighty he truly is! It feels so good to be free that you almost don't acknowledge the freedom of what is… Freedom is the rest; freedom opens the door for you to be able to have the opportunity to have sight in a place that you were blinded to. It is the opportunity to be you. The opportunity presents itself offering you a better version of yourself. You cannot rest here because this is not a stopping point; it is the point of growth and real change. You can blossom here not being held back by the trial, or the pressures. Being free means to have the pureness back in your belly for hope to abide. You must grow here, growth is the place where all is revealed, you are hallowed, stripped before God.

God brings you here only for you to know that here he does not desire to see you but his own reflection. When his Glory is illuminated he desires to see the reflection of it beaming on you. The hallowing is like a pumpkin you open it, gut it and discard of the remains. You then carve into it what you please. God places a light in the inward man only to have it come up and shine for him to see; such as the pumpkin. God is pleased in knowing that now you are able to bear what he is offering to you. You can bear it without the selfishness of being tearful, but the humility of being thankful to be a servant of a King. If you were called by greatness you would answer, but most don't too afraid of what it might require. This is not a call for a new career this is a call for a new life! The newness comes into place because you realize that the destination was not the place, it was the entering into the desires of God. You cannot be healed and say, "That's it thank you, I think I'll take it easy now." You have to go further knowing that there is so much more that the Lord would like to give to you. The freedom is your rest, not your resting place, but your rest. It is the sigh of relief that something brand new is coming that will offer much more than before.

Chapter 5

The Opening

Openness - The Connection.

How good it is to be aligned in the perfection of Christ Jesus! Once you have come to the reality of what it takes then you can begin, more trials come but you are well equipped. Like I said before I started college again, began a new relationship and started to bloom. As I bloomed the Lord began pruning; 'the clipping of the wings'. I didn't know this is what this was until now but I soon learned. In order to come to the perfected state, all of the residue that the pressures and trials left must be scraped. This process is like that Halloween pumpkin that you carve to present it as you desire it to be. Picture the tool that the pumpkin carver is using having two sides. On one side is a spoon, and on the other is the scraper. The scraper is used to dig what wouldn't come easily; a smooth surface! The Lord calls for a smooth surface that he can fill with his majesty. The residue is what was left behind. I was healed from hurt but the residue of that was mistrust. I was healed from abuse but the residue of that was the fear of being beaten. My heart was opened in the boldness of what the new offered, but that old man kept reminding me of the things that had already died as if they still were! So, God turned the spoon and revealed himself as the scraper. The Lord put me in places to be ministered to by his people so that I could get to know him. God always knew me but I did not have a clue that he wanted to share himself with me.

I had to do an internship during a semester in college while studying to be a social worker. I really wanted to get an internship that dealt with women that had been abused. At the time, I was pregnant so it worked out with me interning at a pregnancy resource center. This internship took me to a new understanding. The supervisor that I was under was very chipper, and enthusiastic about the Lord. I had never met people like that before; she would always smile, and was overall just good. During this internship, I witnessed young and old women come in and be given the option of being ministered to. The purpose was to offer them an alternative rather than choosing to abort their child. After ministering she would give them the option of prayer. I was so amazed by this I could not believe that there were people actually doing this.

I would sit and be so emotional by the stories that I heard, some people were so willing to just to have someone pray. I sat stunned nervously awaiting my turn. In one meeting, she allowed me to participate in the leading of prayer. During this prayer, I felt a stillness in the air. I didn't say much but when I lifted my head I could see the expressions dazed by the power of God even at a low level.

I sat meekly, completely still in what I had no knowledge of. Only to come to realize that he had all the knowledge that he needed on me.

During this time, the Lord was courting me as a man does his bride. It's like when a gentleman sees a woman from a far and positions himself in a distance. The man sits watching her attentively. He sends her anonymous flowers at her workplace, and stares at her from a far. He sits quietly watching the sweet reaction on her face when she brags on the beauty of what she has been given. Soon he gets closer and introduces himself as a friend. He listens to her circumstances and what she's been through. Then as she begins to let go of her past and trust him he decides to comfort her. This is when I received the Holy Ghost!

Chapter 6

The Filling

The Filling- The beginning.

My then fiancé would tell me about Jesus and about the Holy Ghost. I had no idea what this was, meanwhile I had my tattoos and skin-tight jeans on. So, the Lord put me in the unbearable! The unbearable is circumstances that either you die or yield. My husband and I would fight almost every weekend to the point it almost became the inevitable. He would try to minister to me but I had no real understanding of what I had to do with Gods plan. Soon events began to happen and my soul was quickened by God. I had dreams where the enemy would come and taunt me. I would be awake and sleep at the same time. I would kick my husband under the covers pleading for him to wake up and help me, but to no avail. I was all alone calling on the name of my husband. One late night while resting a spirit came to me and mocked the Lord and told me, "You're not of God, you think you're of God?" I had no answer, what could I say? I used to be afraid of these things because I was not familiar with this depth of the Lord. In this place, there was no holds barred, he allowed things to come almost to show what the options were. God began to make known to me the warfare over me as clear as day.

My husband and I decided to go to Nashville on another occasion, promising not to have another incident like last time. We headed down praying to have a good time all the while still remembering the events from our last trip there. We got there and all of the sudden it was as if my eyes had been opened like never before. All of these people were on the roads walking, it was pitch black outside and the crowd moved like a flock. These bats were flying over their heads and not one of them ducked they just kept walking as if it were normal. I looked over to my husband and spoke, "night walkers," he turned and looked at me with the eyes of the Lord.

It was as if he watched the gift of discernment birth itself right before his eyes. I didn't know then it was discernment. When we got to the hotel I looked out of the window amazed that I could actually see the spirit of the living dead. I stayed in the hotel room and had no interest in partaking in anything that could entangle me with what I had seen. I was being made over by God. It was a quickening of what God had planned all along. I got back home and an interest in the Lord began to saturate my thoughts, I had so many questions and no answers. I was in a service one night and heard the pastor say, "If you come back tonight you will receive the Holy Ghost." I kissed my husband and children goodbye and headed straight to church. I tried to get it but was not able to receive him; defeated and hurt I went back home. All the while the Lord was watching, drawing me with a pull I had never felt before. The circumstances became so hard with my spouse that I had decided to stop drinking. I never drank heavily, but my husband didn't handle his liquor well so I said I would stop to help him stop. We would argue so much that almost every weekend the police were called; they almost knew us by name. Still the Lord was watching, see this place is pivotal. It is like the peak of pain where so much happens all at once. It seems there is no other way but to give up or fight to the death.

The day I was baptized I was dressed in all white, no one warned me about the temperature of the water; I had never felt water this cold. After I was pulled up I was so happy. I didn't know what happened but I knew a change had occurred. I got home and my husband and I started to call on Jesus. My husband began speaking in a language I didn't know and I felt so discouraged that he had received what I was seeking. I heard what could have been the Lord say, "Separate". I got up and my husband hugged me and told me it was okay. When he let me go I felt a heaviness rest on me as I was brought to humility, I screamed, "JESUS!" I began speaking in a language I didn't know, I couldn't stop it, it just flowed as my husband stood there watching me. It wasn't my husband at all it was the Lord witnessing the perfected work of his hands, and how the potency of his Love drew me to his fire. Everything that I had gone through during that time had literally walked me right into the arms of the Lord.

Chapter 7

The Release

The Release - All.

The Lord requires all, not some but much. The place of the release welcomed me during the trial of circumstances. The things that the Lord brought before introduced and actually catapulted me into the release. A release is when he opens himself to you. It's not like a man extending their arm, reaching out at the length of their abilities. I'm talking about Jesus!

I grew up with my grandmother, but as I went off to college I got myself into rocky situations. At that time when I went through things I would close up. It would be periods when no one could reach me and for a long time, I regretted that. My grandmother and I were like two peas in a pod. My grandmother knew me inside and out. So even though I was distant she knew me well enough to know that the time would come when I would be back. My Mema was a very confident and diligent woman. She was able to hold her own, oxygen tank and all. It came a time when age dealt its hand and she had become more ill than I knew, but in the meantime the Lord was working on a miracle… While I was about 7 months pregnant, I only had one vehicle and 3 children that filled it, with the fourth on the way. We didn't have the funds for a car seat let alone an extra vehicle. I hadn't been back home to St. Louis for about a year, and had been very distant from family. I seemed to always be caught up in my own affairs.

My husband searched high and low for a SUV, frustrated with the prices, he almost gave up. For some reason I had peace, I barely even took a glance to see what the internet said because I knew somehow it would work out. Don't ask me where this peace came from because back then I couldn't tell you, but now I know.

My husband and I had been fussing at one another when a contest called Living Radiantly popped across the screen. It was a commercial for B.E.T. networks. The contest required a paragraph or so about what you went through and how you came out of it living radiantly. I decided to enter it not paying attention to the prizes. I showed my husband my entry but he paid it no mind. A few weeks later I had gotten really ill during my pregnancy so my husband had to do just about everything for me. Which was amazing, he was very helpful. This was our first child together, and his first child period. The other 3 children were from my previous relationship that I spoke about earlier.

On a cold winter day driving home from class I noticed I had a voicemail. I checked my voicemail, and sure enough it was a representative from B.E.T. networks. The voicemail stated that I needed to claim my prize of $10,000.00. I was so in shock and could barely catch my breath. I was in such awe of the moment I was speechless. My husband and I just looked at one another and cried without words to say.

This is the positioning of God. This is where things align themselves with what you prayed for, and what the Lord desires. The Lord illuminated a vehicle for an amount we could purchase. We could have no other way afforded if it wasn't for this divine interception by the hand of God. The S.U.V. was just what we needed, and it was located in St. Louis Mo. We had to travel to St. Louis (my hometown) to purchase it. I can remember receiving the check and trying to cash it at a bank, still in shock of what I was holding. The bank teller told me it wasn't real and that she couldn't cash it. Disheartened I went outside and told my husband. We then went to another bank and received a completely different response. The teller called me to the back room, offered me a drink and showed great interest in my circumstances. I was a student in a social work program holding a $10,000.00 check from B.E.T. for writing. The enemy was so confused because it seemed that all the doors were shut. Really, they were wide open in an area that he had not even seen. So, while he attacked in one place the Lord had already transitioned me to a new place.

The first bank was the old but the new place welcomed me. No man could have prevented what the Lord saw fit to do. See I've learned that sometimes people gage God from what they've seen. They measure you by what you have achieved. Basing your destiny off of what they have seen you do. Never stopping to see that you are being led into the great unknown of what God can do for you. I forgave the first teller because she couldn't understand the blessing, and I forgave the second teller for trying to see things naturally. All along it had nothing to do with me but all to do with what the beginning and the end had already spoke over me! When the Lord has a decree, nothing can hinder or pry in the way. A lot of times we pray for things and are discouraged when they seem to tarry. The understanding of this is that the Lord of Host has already done it all, all you have to do is walk. Pray for those that don't know how to pray for themselves, all the while knowing if you are his it is already worked out for you. As you do you will begin walking in increase. Without seeking but by faith knowing. You don't have to worry because things will occur and you will begin seeing things working for your good.

All along you were praying for things that were not spoken over you. Creating a destiny that was not created to bare the who that he is in you, but the who that you feel you ought to be. That conception is not for your good nor his. If you yield to what does not seem so, that is actually the spirit being quickened by who it knows to be. In the womb, you were already created and desired by God to be a thing so you can do a thing in this realm. Your birthing was not in vain, because in the canal you are prepared for what your journey will be. In the belly, you were being prepared for a desired destination. As you know some children are nurtured and have songs sung to them in the womb. Some are filtered and covered by proper eating and great care. Some are misused and tainted with distractions and drug use. All of this is preparing the seed for the path they were established, and set to conquer here on earth. Nothing in God is in vain.

When Jesus was born look at the circumstances; his mother was a virgin, pure. His father Joseph could not enter into to her, the womb could not be tainted, pure. Jesus was born in spiritual warfare. Jesus was born in a manger with a king desiring his death before he could speak (Luke 2:1-20 KJV). You have to see and understand that in the womb you were established, the birthing told the destiny! As you live the life that is here it chokes out the pureness of what was. Thoughts come of who you could be rather than knowing who you already were when you were in the hallow place of God (the mind). You were prepared even before entering into the womb of your mother. These bank tellers were unaware of this, as was I until the outpouring of the Holy Ghost fell upon me.

My husband and I traveled to St. Louis and purchased the SUV, he was elated. My spirit stayed very calm still waiting to see what the end would be. While visiting my grandmother, I looked at her noticing her frail disposition. I seen her in a rare state, but as I sat with her on her bed she had this great peace. Mostly all of her grandchildren were present which was rare. We sat on her bed as she stared off with a smile that seemed untraceable. As I got up to leave I believe I heard the Lord tell me to go back and hug her again. When I went back she smiled almost surprised that I had come back. My grandmother embraced me sweetly and walked to the door to see our new truck. My husband drove in the new truck with all of the children. I followed behind in the old truck by myself. As I left the house I had a complete breakdown. I cried the whole 2 hours it took to get back home. A strong feeling came over me that I wouldn't see her again.

I pleaded for the Lord to help me be strong. I didn't cry for the miracle that was being driven right in front of me, but I cried for what the Lord had allowed me to see. Surely after getting home a week passed, and while watching T.V. I heard a text come to my phone. When I heard the text alert I knew who it was and what it said. I picked up the phone and quietly headed to the bathroom. The text read that my grandmother had passed away. My soul sighed because of the miracle that God had performed. You are blessed if you can see that the blessing was the money. The miracle was that I heard and seen before time. So, when it came to pass my heart would not faint but had already been covered and kept by the hand of God. I was able to continue on journeying with him. I was able to come to the who that he is with no regret of what could have, or should have been done. I had been given peace, and all was well in our parting.

The cash prize came but the second part of the prize never came, they told me that a life coach would fly out to meet with me, but they never spoke about it again. I believe that she couldn't come because my life was already coaching me.

Chapter 8

The Fullness

Fullness- Entirety

Growing up I was a seemingly strange child, I would yearn for something that seemed unattainable. I always kept to myself, afraid to open up because of what was outside of the opening. I went through my life being molded by the events that entered into the path that I was on. Every time a change came I shifted. My core remained but the outward man conformed to what the appearance of what presented itself was. I was in a shell somewhat shut in. I could accomplish things, but never wanting to go past that place of safety in myself. The Lord watched me yield to his trials, and overcome the circumstances. All the while victory stood beside me declaring to everything that was sent, "Get behind thee for it is written.... a mighty conqueror she shall be. None shall defeat her nor make her afraid!" I walked aimlessly not knowing the dangers that I faced. Not even recognizing the great love of heaven that sought me. I never seen me as me, just a shell of time walking in the earth.

I knew happiness was close but it always seemed to be hiding from me. I would sit crying in despair, hopeless to when my end would be. I never knew where that emptiness came from, or why I just couldn't seem to lay hold to happiness like everyone else. Most seemed motivated by the hope of success, or the things that wealth brought. Some even seemed satisfied with vain things of what seemed even though they knew that they weren't. I would sit and see their smiles, asking myself is it me? Are they true to what they have sought? Is happiness available to everyone but me? Then the Lord revealed to me that the seeking is the happiness. The seeking is the journey. The understanding of the seeking is the difference of who and what you're seeking it for. I never even knew why I sought this so dearly. The Lord showed me in my later years that it was him that I sought. It was the love that others could not quench. It was him all along; Jesus in me sought Jesus in him.

The joy that I sought was not the smallness of a smile but the filling of eternal hope. I had come to a resting place never to be born again, but to be born again in him! He is, so I am happy! My spirit could not rest, it could never settle with just a false sense of compliments. Compliments being given by those who seen what they could hold, and held what they could grab, hoping that what they attained was what they had sought.

All of the places I had been through were simply to pick up, and to give back. Laying hold to the things that would equip me in readiness. Then giving back everything that I picked up knowing that what I needed I already had. This is the fullness. You have everything the moment that God Almighty breathes upon you in his strength. Knowing that once his presence was offered unto you, you became full with all. Simply because all is already given. Jesus is the beginning and the end, so he does not send his sheep for the slaughter into a place full of sinful entireties. Jesus prepares you beforehand. He is, so you are entirely full upon entrance. The suffering and seeking comes from having to come to what you already knew before you were brought forth out of the womb. Seeing a new face and a new plan, only to realize the plan had already been established for you to be full and seek no more!

Chapter 9

The Real

The Real- The out flow of what is...

What is it? What is purpose that we would seek it? Is it destiny? The desires of our hearts? Is it a place that we would look after once we have attained it? Purpose is what comes before knowledge. It comes as a thought, an idea of what could be in the hopes of what is. Could I be that? I believe I could do that. These are the thoughts that come in to take hold, when really no thought can be given if you are seeking the purposeful seed. The purpose is a time, simply a moment of what came and is no more. It is in the greatness of what was declared and the basics of what has been done, then it can become real.

I seen greatness in those around me often but never seen it upon myself. I believe the Lord spoke back to me and allowed me to know, "If you see it you've only seen the error of what this place has revealed. If you cannot attain the sight of what lies upon thee then surely greatness is with you." True greatness does not identify itself it just is. Geniuses never proclaim or declare, they are outed or acknowledge by another as they just are. They work diligently with their feet kept and there head low. A soft whisper says, "Look," as they are timidly working. A stranger takes heed of the greatness shown on the humble stature of those who never stopped to see. The greatness that is poured upon you is not the vison you can hold. True greatness is discovered, and then declared for what is. It is not noticeable to the portion but revealed to the masses.

When Harriet Tubman decided to escape no one had seen how great it really was; her small frame being weighed by the destiny that was upon her. Rosa Parks had not decided her purpose but in an instant, in a real moment the rawness of her possibilities was shown for all to see. It seemed to manifest in an instant of lowliness brought for the purposeful seed. Greatness is the unknown, the unreachable. If you can complete your vision you don't have vision at all. The truth knows that greatness has no end or beginning. Truth lies in Jesus where truth reveals the truth that all things are possible, there is no end. Greatness is revealed by a move, a mighty shift. The realness is knowing that when you know greatness, the purposeful seed (The person) has already served and is no more. It is only to be seen when the greatness has manifested and reveals what soil it was really rooted in.

Chapter 10

"Delivering Me"

Delivering Me- Who is it that you say that I am? (Mark 8:27-30, KJV)

All of this time I had been believing that I knew who I was, sure that my understanding was full. Really, I was full of myself, I was lacking the very thing that could have built the foundation of the truth in my inward parts. I had to be delivered! I had to be brought out of what seemed to be my thoughts and understand that these thoughts were none of mine. They were simply the images of what had been portrayed by what others had thought of me. I had received them lost without direction, not realizing that they were sent purposely to detour me. These perceptions could have seared me from the who that was imbedded in me before time. Nothing else mattered but to be free of this. Being free of this meant coming to the reality of the truth that became a lie within me. The lie of what I had been told all along. The Lord showed me a better version of myself. I could have never fathomed that what God seen was not a version but the true me. Though life emulates, and deceives it is something within that already knows. I had known but I didn't know, this is where the deliverance must come.

You must be delivered from this life so you can live. Life is a version, a facade of what could be. It's only accomplished in the heavens to bring down into the earth, and push them to pass yourself. Simply by the leading, and unctioning of the Holy Ghost given by the prosperity of God.

Once I had come to this place I realized that I had come, but did not know what to do. I was still the same seemingly, but something had shifted in me. I desired to reach and attain something that I otherwise could have in no way even been able to hold. It's like in a relationship; you meet someone who is drawn to you by your apparel, shape, character, or appearance. As time goes on the affection may fade, then you are stuck trying to figure out how do I change this? How do make the love return to me? But if the love was established here on earth, its foundation wasn't built on the things of heaven. When you are made over by God the affection grows, it becomes heightened. Even as time goes he endears you as if it was the first time. God is the heights of heaven and the valleys on earth. When you are courted and he sees himself upon you, you must be stripped, hallowed, and delivered. He looks upon you knowing that it is himself, recognizing the works of his hands. Through time you have been told, "This is cute, that fits, you should keep that." However, when Jesus comes he draws out what's within so no offence comes by what he has to pull off. The deliverance is necessary and very crucial to what God has intended. Without a new mind and a refreshed spirit, the looks of another man may come and draw you away. Making you believe that this time with God was only a phase. Only a set time that you could have had the possibility of retaining his image. So, after he has washed you, you must be renewed coming into the Know.

You must know that you are, so you can be who you are. If you have on a pretty dress, and have cleaned up then you step out and someone says, "Oh my why did you do that to your hair?" Then the wind blows against you and unfluffs a curl. Deliverance gives you the ability to be able to understand the know, that you are confident and unmoved. Then you become sturdy in Christ. A vessel set to be used knowing that all things are waiting for the arrival of your manifestation. Now Jesus can adorn you as he pleases without holding back. As he draws you closer a shift is required otherwise you are only drawn for a moment. The Lord desires for you to be drawn eternally.

Once you have come then deliverance is seen. Deliverance carries away the old and brings forth the new. The new can become old if you have no understanding of what to do with it. The understanding is this, who is it that you say that I am? Perfected wisdom in the next place. This question is rhetorical as if you're drawing out the enemies in your past. Calling them and the thoughts they have toward you out. Only to dismiss them; all the while keeping the who that you know that you are without even blinking an eye. Almost like saying you know who I am, and what I am able to do, don't limit with the hopes that you see. My sight is not predetermined by man, it is consecrated in heaven by the creator. My creator knows that as he is as am I! No man can determine this thing unless it is by the spirit and if by the spirit; it is unspoken because the spirit knows all things.

I have come to a place in my life of great confusion. This place did not frighten me because it was for the edification of my thoughts toward thought. I would sometimes think things and plead the Blood. Or things would slip out of my mouth only to realize that those were the truths of my soul. I ran from these things thinking how could I have thought that? I would sometimes sound so stern, so potent, so unlike me. The Lord showed me, it is not for the eyes to determine the speech it is for the spirit to speak for the mind. Therefore, being without thought. Thought keeps the things that are held pleading for release. Truth has to purge the inner parts that would have no other way been cleaned if it wasn't for the pureness of God's spirit.

I would hear the depths sometimes as I spoke and it would sound intimidating even to me. I would say, "Oh my goodness Lord forgive me, I don't know where that came from?" I had become so used to the meek, mild mannered, and suffered child that I had grown accustom with. Boldness would come and then I would cause it to succumb with the doubts of that can't be, but it was. I was so used to my voice not being heard that when I heard it was unrecognizable even to me. I would speak and feel the authority; I would move and hear the boldness of the realms around me. I felt a shift when I spoke the truths given to me. It was always the times when I was just able to let go, and be free when I really felt the Lord. God would speak to my spirit and say, "Well done." The Lord delivered me and as I was reborn. I had to accommodate the occupancy of the fleshy mind, until the appointed time for me to truly be in Christ.

He set me free from all that I used to know, all that I believed, and my old thoughts. All that I knew is no more and I won't ever call it back because it has come to cease. I am free of it, I have grown to welcome change. When you say your changed or you have been made whole, you come to find that people watch you. They watch waiting for you to reveal to them the seen difference. It is not for them to see, it is for them to know.

When Jesus uncovered the blind man, he allowed the man to see. The man saw what he chose to see. The first time the man saw by the spirit, eventually he gained the sight of the flesh. (Mark 8:24, KJV) When your change is revealed all eyes will be uncovered to behold all that God has delivered you from, and all God has brought you to.

I have learned a lot during this time in my life. I have learned ultimately how to suffer in the firmament of God's glory. This suffering has been an uphill battle but it has definitely been worth it. I have recognized great feats in my life, strongholds, and yokes some refusing to let me go but the Blood of Jesus. The Lord has cleaned me, and journeyed with me allowing me the knowledge of all these things. Ultimately, I have come this far only to realize that I am in the perfect place to pray!

Our Father which art in heaven, hallowed be thy name. Thy kingdom come thy will be done in earth, as it is in heaven. Give us this day our daily bread and forgive us our trespasses, as we forgive those who trespass against us. Lead us not into temptation but deliver us from evil. For thine is the kingdom, the power, and the glory forever and ever!

Thank you, JESUS!

Author Biography

The Perfect Place To Pray delivers a fresh and new approach to listening and hearing God's voice. By mixing modern day predicaments with an understanding that comes forth like wisdom from the Old Testament, Angel Clove will help you better recognize God's will and guidance in your life. *The Perfect Place To Pray* is the perfect read for those who want to grow in their faith journey.

Angel Clove initially lived with her mother, and then later moved in with her grandmother by the age of sixteen. Now a wife and mother to four beautiful children, Angel hopes you will enjoy and learn from her personal journey. She prays you will grow in your faith by knowing how God led her–as He did for her, God will do for you.

www.ingramcontent.com/pod-product-compliance
Lightning Source LLC
Chambersburg PA
CBHW032051180726
48284CB00004B/1290
9781945976568